The Village of Sliding Time

Books by David Zieroth

The Village of Sliding Time (2006)

The Education of Mr. Whippoorwill: A Country Boyhood (2002)

Crows Do Not Have Retirement (2001)

How I Joined Humanity at Last (1998)

The Weight of My Raggedy Skin (1991)

When the Stones Fly Up (1985)

Mid-River (1981)

Clearing: Poems from a Journey (1973)

The Village of Sliding Time

DAVID ZIEROTH

HARBOUR PUBLISHING
MADEIRA PARK, BC
2006

Harbour Publishing
P.O. Box 219
Madeira Park, BC V0N 2H0
www.harbourpublishing.com

Edited by Silas White

Harbour Publishing acknowledges the financial support of the
Government of Canada through the Canada Council for the Arts and
the Book Publishing Industry Development Program (BPIDP), and
from the Province of British Columbia through the British Columbia
Arts Council and the Book Publisher's Tax Credit through the Ministry
of Provincial Revenue.

Printed and bound in Canada.

LIBRARY AND ARCHIVES CANADA CATALOGUING IN PUBLICATION

Zieroth, David

  The village of sliding time / David Zieroth.

A poem.

ISBN 1-55017-388-X

  I. Title.

PS8599.I47V54 2006   C811'.54   C2006-900284-3

"Love takes one's neighbour as one's other self,
and loves him with all the immense humility and
discretion and reserve and reverence without
which no one can presume to enter into the
sanctuary of another's subjectivity."

–Thomas Merton, *The Wisdom of the Desert*

"Now you understand why people live in villages,
sniffing at their neighbours' cooking and their
conversations. They fear themselves and what
could happen if the leash were cut and they were
all alone."

–Jim Crace, *The Gift of Stones*

"So little happens; the black dog
Cracking his fleas in the hot sun
Is history . . .

Stay, then, village, for round you spins
On slow axis a world as vast
And meaningful as any poised
By great Plato's solitary mind."

–R. S. Thomas, "The Village"

HOW I CAME TO BE

1.

One March night my folks
took themselves to bed
and found inside their comfort
some love left
She curled after
picturing a daughter to complement
two sons and one girl already
behind other walls, asleep
He flung his arm
and drifted, seeing chores
that lay ahead, the seeding
far enough away to contemplate
with pleasure because this season
was still long although
yesterday he had seen the first crow
and felt his mood lift

But what of *me* between
these two: why pick them
from among the multitudes
meeting and begetting that very night
(an early-morning tilt when a freight
banged by and half awoke
two slippery reaching dreamers
or the tired sore workers
who found nothing but this moment
of sharing and saying wild words
to steady them for one more shift
or the young, young pretty ones
whose trembling bore them
past that point they had
so often been forewarned about
—history now, sad or otherwise
is hard yet to say)
Instead I came here, to these limbs
this farm, these white fields
swept with a snaky wind

2.

All that summer my mother
carried me through the heat
and when I recognized winter again
by the soft slow nights
I knew it was time to show them
who I was

although I could not reveal
who I had been
before taking spirit handfuls
from each: his ears, her heart

              —but from neither
my need for snow: that was my own
desire, that would be the tiny bit
I carried on my own—

                      and my first
and frequent cries that followed
kept them from fretting
about the cold, remembering always
to press me near and warm

Only now and then was I left
by the window where ice
leapt with the draft upon the pane
into filaments of shine and angle
recalling I could be
no longer
that cool bright light of
almost emptiness
so entirely filled
with more than me

THE VILLAGE OF SLIDING TIME

An early morning
knock on my apartment door
it is myself, a younger
teenaged boy
come to take me back

and guide me through
what I had thought gone
but no, he says, look
(his palms up, his face
open) I can make

anyone you want to see
walk down this hall
and into your arms—
your mum, your dad
your old dog, friends

    (how to decide
    when the maps
    are not set out
    to read with ease
    though I tried
    through dozens of days
    the calamities of seasons
    hands on sunbright hair and head
    to catch my parents' looks
    over a homemade card
    Mother glances at
    the question
    Father turns from
    what he did back

when he lived alone
before learning unselfishness
among the nest of us)

my younger self
grins on in
youthful rosy certitude
doesn't see
how far I've come
from his age
how I'm hiding
just these thoughts

under my moustache
whereas his clean upper lip
simply shines
he keeps saying: tell me
who you want to see

I have the gift
of sliding time
under your slippers
he says: wish, sing out

he stands straight
his cap tipped back
his hair lush
cut crookedly but not
so he seems to notice

or care, and admittedly
he charms me
the clear face, his pleasant
insistence
on his might

to make me see
what once I lived
and where
so I am suddenly unnerved
till he reaches out

and stills my qualms
he's had his own disputes
some I remember
he's come a long way
to offer a journey

I can't make alone
so off to Lonsdale Avenue
our elbows knocking
gaits aligned, old hammer and new
down the hall

with its smells, dry leaves, petals
plastic candy wrappers
dropped by children
near the stacks of
newspapers waiting for someone

to let them in
Old Nick, twenty years
in the block, his wife dead
for ten, lived in army huts
where Cap Mall now stands
building
his sorrowful stories
stopped for the ambulance
or the ambulance stopped for him
a toque on his head
though it was summer
his hands blue
which asked my own blood
to re-measure itself
in view of his grip on the chrome
bar of the stretcher
his freezing feet
(one of the feet stories)
the bent curved feet
of the old, the soft boneless
limbs of babies . . .

to draw the boy closer
I mention those his age
the cadets gathering
to play metal tunes
glockenspiel marching

a flat-roofed Navy League
bunker, drums breaking
bylaws and still the sergeant
shouts
a bald man bulging blue
his face some days

harshly pink
his shoes so black
his belt too tight
younger than me
but like an uncle

in the smelly room
a small boy beside him
inelegant in step *left left*
left right left
can't swing his arms

in tempo but who's
going to laugh
or sneer or shout, not
that short kid
stumbling

on his laces, he'll never get
to bang the snare
under the sergeant's favoured
stare, be the young one
who comes early

to open the bunker
transform himself
into a crisp pressed youth
not like the tenant in the
penthouse throwing his bedding

out the window in the night
nor like Buck (here for
seventeen years) whose mattress fire
drives out the resident manager
and five others, fleeing . . .

the boy stops
surprised
and then smiles
moves his hand

I jump down
into the squeaky snow
and look around
horses and cutters
more than trucks and cars
a livery stable where men
piss with geldings and mares
a store
my mother on one side
Eva on the other
friends beyond
exchange of flour
sugar and salt
then the storm blocks
the road home, trapping

my brother and me
in town late in the day
close to night and the plough
far away, the road at first
a groove through the field
now plugged hard white
while we wait
I kneel on the floor
thumb comics, the bad
and good guys don't matter
just the colour
and the varied balloons
where characters speak simply
till Eva says
Don't look if you can't buy
and I hate her
for not including me
in her friendship
with my mother
blasted away as she whisks by
in her tight clothes and short hair
I have to get home
my brother, older
already spinning the family car
to and from school
has to get home more:
to stay at Eva's turns back
his dream of adulthood
working for Jack Gardner
all hay season, chucking
bales over his head
—so when the plough arrives

we follow its light
through the dark that comes
after
a storm, the driver
throwing up milk waves
pouring them onto other waves
and we feel the gravel again
under our tires all the way home
Father feeding pigs
Mother surprised to see us
already on the phone
to thank and talk
except the line is busy

is often static fuzzy-blur
yet sometimes now slips
into nicker of a horse
the wet feathers, a grey hen
grasshoppers overhead
sweat, snow, dung, white sky
ice in the trough, ticks on a dog
forks in a heap
thud of dirt on a box
and my mind layering
slow, fast, then stopped
by the skyful of Orion's
belt of jewels
so plainly strewn
and long used for
making children gape
and grope toward
what can't be touched . . .

the boy smiles
and opens his hands
so I speculate about
what skills of his
I've lost, what thrills

in his heart run out
and meet in the air
manifestations so perfect
they become holy for an hour
natural, expected

like clouds on a good day
going by pleasantly, there
but not a worry
even the future
may have to meet

I tell him
something collects around
the strange sounds
from another apartment
a shout or cry

filters through a wall
would he grasp
that slippery moment
I turn from my book
and then relax back into

my own spinning self
would he tilt his head
he's never slept
away, always the same bed

same moonlight on his cheek
whippoorwill tugging up
his dreams of dogs
and days of playing
with frogs, in ditches
leaping in and out of warm mud . . .

he opens his hands
to include Edgar
striding down to Emma
in her blue house
three kids of her own
and a husband dead in the war
it is said and we knew
when the story ended
she had loved Edgar
though he told stories in the pub
of her spongy bed

his brother Delbert
born with the horses
and running his Arabian
past the kids
in the sandy schoolyard
leaving with the circus and getting killed
in Montana, so far from home
it was a myth

Montana's coolness in August
turns him
to face the mountain
to catch its chill
a bullet
outside the circle we had drawn
no farther than
the first big city, finding
work and the trouble
of not knowing
women, his brothers
randy as well
wearing their boots, swearing
at the dances
all elbows up to the girls
who shied away, sensing
in that heat
some ache too big
driving him outside
to drink
and scuff up dirt
behind the cars
punching a rival who sauntered
out of the happy hall into the night
the shouting and sudden whap
of fist on face, dust rising
and the circle forming
screaming on the outside
until someone's down
and when the kicking starts
men close in, the shiner
already growing

later word came back
he broke the bank somewhere
his luck manic till the end
the manager sure he was cheating
at cards
and later his body returned
down from that coolness
into the corner of a quarter section
its tidy fence
against which the summer
beat until the wood went white

And so the boy and I thought:
was this the way out?
to live a crazed life, early
memorable death
a gun involved
(one of the gun stories)
could we claim our real life
while everyone knew
we had to fight off the skin
we were born in
shed it—get
stylish, witty
sincere and complete
able to wear a hat
or not, undergo winter
with no wool scarf
equal to the brunt of cold
such a man
our family has never seen
growing in a mind

where others never thought
to look

... and finding Tillie
still not eating
at the fowl suppers
wouldn't take the sandwiches
unless they were her own
afraid always of
the unspeakable fact
someone had touched her food
and making enemies
because everyone knew
she threw eggshells
and tin cans out her kitchen door
the place so rank
few had ever seen it

but those who did
were sharp of eye and keen
tellers, this story anyway
happy to accept
the imagination of the community
they were mostly not unkind
but some days not so tired either
they couldn't adapt and
improvise, whether on the phone
or stopped on village streets

and though her husband
was shadowy on another section

and her girl tall
and quick, she herself was a witch
her hair pulled back
a steel knot and her smell
and her wild way of talking
and the hump of her car
(though her weak and smiling son
was kind
to little kids and never
played baseball, some age
or lung exemption in effect
the teacher standing with him
on the edge of the diamond
if he hadn't been called home
through the stony pasture)
hers the only farm
to keep sheep
other farmers clucked about
called them a danger
an impertinence
not choosing beef and grain
held to by the Z family
the K family . . .

I'll call out the names of
Judy and Frank
Heinz and Tony
Rowena
Olga
Lydia
        Adolf

. . . the S family
lived at the outside edge
of the circle, a grey house
holding a fat mother
skinny father and
seven children plus one ghost
I was drawn to
by the girls'
slow telling: one night
they were awakened
out of their bed where two slept
when another, not quite
the youngest, walked somnolent
and then screamed
at the top of the worn wood
steps, their mother
flapping with a blanket around her
to scare off
what the child swore later
she saw
grey and white and eyes
drew her forward
where she was compelled
to fall and break her neck
on the stairs
though no word was said
until she flickered and her mother
grabbed her
this time the ghost most
demanding, and when I asked
what it wanted from Pauline

no one said
they went home
on the sandy roads to
the last farm
without electricity, and I begged
to see what could not be seen
in daylight
and never by the males
those big boys went
silent around arithmetic and then
fainted when the public nurse
arrived with needles
and finally they took me
inside the house where colour
was missing, the oil cloth
washed-out white, only
a pale fringe
of flowers
and the mother in her chair
eyeing me coldly
while her daughters guided me
upstairs and said, there, go up
and you'll see
what we've been saying, there's
nothing to see
you have to sleep here
and even so I went up a ways
feeling along the wall
until I came in sight of
the landing and saw
not the ghost but the bundle of clothes
a family of nine produces

and noticed for the first time
the rags they wore
the old man's overalls and the
dresses made and remade
out of which
so much desire would arise . . .

and the boy set out
to grasp shadows
and make them vanish
      walking home
on the road that ran always
perpendicular to fields
a vague ditch at the side
fence and posts guiding him
down the road itself
so little used
quack grass
in the middle where tires
seldom crushed
and above him
the always swaying poplars
wind and wood
framing for him
the deer family
out of the bush and staring
their tawny sides
dappled in saskatoon light
one two three they flew
over the top wire and gone
turning this way and that
through trees as if they knew

a path he could never find
though he'd look, waiting
for some sign, sure the grasses
would release more than ticks
deflected uprushing grouse
sounding off
through branches
not much direction just the drive
to get away from him
perhaps its nest near and again
he'd look and feel sure
he'd find what he hunted for
some new noun to arrange
neatly on the mind's wall
until the mixture of the world
was correctly known
the way a crow walked
the coming of the snow each year
smoothness inside the swallow's nest
heartbeat of a dog, stink
of a skunk in spring, wet sack
of kittens . . .

but someone is saying
a soul can form
beyond sun-blasted villages
and clay-hard roads
so-flat-you-had-to-flee
fields
your tender loving
looking back cannot make me see

someone wants more than
testimonial
parts cohering now and then
into shudders—
wants brutal immediate relevance

       that no one spoke of
at the canasta evenings
deep in winter, card tables
propped around the stove
backed up against
the donna-conna walls
when everyone knew who would
win: Myrtle
with the Matinee hanging
from her lip, the way she
calculated every card
and after every round told us
how we could've played
the black ace or the red
queen, the noise of table talk
growing louder though no one
called it cheating
and no one cared
who won
all glad for
the chatter
of friends and the surprise
of numbers and cards and then
tea in mugs and oatmeal cookies
and cinnamon rolls and fresh

buns
and cucumber pickles fetched up
from the cellar off the shelf
rows of preserves
and homemade chokecherry wine
saved for
a wedding when city relatives
came driving out
in long cars, their fins
cutting the air
and the fat ones
offering scotch
to my mother

would you like
a nightcap?

no thanks she said
she always wore a hairnet
to bed

country mice

hilling potatoes, staking tomatoes
shelling peas into great
shiny bowls on the front steps
telling stories of even
older people and their unhappy
lives
when they'd left Europe
never to return and re-enter
the house where they were born

children who played
in the sand by the door
little guttural sounds as their hands
went through the trails of dirt
looking up, squinting at
a shadow, an old one
a thin grandfather
fat gramma
each pushing a stick
into the ground, dead
any time God wanted to test
their faith
they kept up
their tongues (German
Ukrainian, Polish) so I couldn't
tell one from another
back of the café, though
some old women blew snot
out their noses
and some did not . . .

a city looker
has never seen such dirt
grimed around the knuckles
the nails ribbed, cuticles
ripped far from polish
yet every child
loves the touch
at the end of the day
from the hand
that wrings the rooster's neck,
reaches in

for the wet heart, the gizzard
tossed to gulping dogs, kidneys kept back
for a husband's sweetheart stew

Harry always rolling his own
and no guns in his home
he borrowed what he needed
I was there
when his sons pulled
the heifer out of the barn
and manoeuvred her
so Harry could place the blow
accurately swinging the axe
onto the white curls
of her forehead
deep dull noise
my astonishment
at the value of a gun
the distance Harry
hadn't needed, willing to go
one-on-one with the young
he'd raised, and how we knew
he loved all his sons
though he was offhand, choked
his boys already talking past him
and into the car
Harry knew they needed
the advantage each of his too many sons
would present to women
red Merc so necessary
to woo the daughters
of the neighbours

driving one home
from dancing
hoping hints in the waltz
suggested futures in the car
—and her counting on her hair
to attract a man, someone
she wouldn't mind if his hand
slipped
the sex play risky
because the girls really were
looking for the best guy
to get them out of town
into the city, some
teenaged marriages entirely
the championing
of adolescent lust
unable to imagine the world
in what the books said
and Harry anyway
not able to read
yet not worried about
going into town
he seldom sat long
and only if he talked
about this field or that
farmer if he talked at all
at one point the big house
too small for all the beds
required, the featherticks
holding off the cold
pinching the longjohns
so someone went down

into the kitchen
smelling of milk
to light the stove
and then Harry'd get up
only twice in his life
at the dentist, once to pull
what remained of his teeth, then
to get the new set, which meant
he mostly went
without, not bothering
to cover his mouth
when he laughed
learning to chew in a new way
living for the day he could
collect a pension
a boon for the hardy
a prize from Parliament
if you can stand the cold
and the heat and the wind
made him wear
too many clothes or scarcely any
the bits of hay sticking
in summer when he
hiked up forkfuls into the loft
wild flowers, sweat
and horse, each family
possessing a tinge of sourness
from clothes too long
held upstairs
in the attic
between planks of wood
the rows of vermiculite

this compound
kills them, someone discovers
later—old perils rolling around
above their scalps
unlike now: every chemical
on probation
then they stuck hands in
malathion
dithiocarbamate
stinking . . .

but no one smelled like
the half-breed who came to trap
the ditch for muskrat, stopping in
to ask for work, muscular
his wife back by the truck
two kids, no dog for them
going to the ditch to camp
off-road, clay
so slippery in the spring
you had to walk
the ring of his tent
held down by rocks
and the fire a circle of stones
with a few bones
from something that once
passed through his hands
and died
they ate it
and went to sleep on the ground
blankets sufficient to keep off

the morning chill, the smoke
darkening his red
handkerchief sometimes
around his head
or on his neck, his face hard to read
and his voice low
not trusting what he might say
not sure he would be heard
sure he would be leaving
once he trapped out the ditch
and left with the oily skins
he could parlay into money
I saw their tent for a week
from my bedroom window
far off at the point
beyond which I couldn't see
and then they were gone
I fingered the charred
sticks left behind
in their camp, nomads
never worried about
seeds washed away
or choked out, blown to
a neighbour's field
they went back to the lake
where I watched them
later in the summer on their side
of the beach, bulrushes
different from our shore
the lake snakes six feet long
swimming past the naked
brown babies dropped

in the sand and dragging
their wet bottoms into
the warm milky water
everything they did slow
in retreat as if
each wave lapping up
needed to be seen
and maybe measured
while the people
in my party ran
in and out, this treat
of the lake only twice a summer
wading out till the water
lifted armpits
toes like eyes sorting
slime from sand, shaking both
from our towels

parts of other bodies
not normally seen, breasts
on some men, hair
on women and the bulges
unusually outlined in wet

only the old men staying
under the poplars to smoke
slowly saying the obvious
about the heat
the way the lake went
over the edge of the world
and left a grey line
not the see-saw of old tree/

young tree with
airborne swallows
or the slower filling up
of snow, these men
shared tools, stories
tobacco, bulls and boars
and lived together
though miles apart
five miles from town
versus twenty

space between farms
makes a family see
a dusty car
drive into the yard
bearing fellowship
sometimes kids'
toys, thoughts new
and shiny

and scattered
here and there a bachelor
without books
lived in the kitchen
one broken couch
in the dark, the last visitor
a census taker
his own sister never coming
now she'd got away
into one of the towns
stepping stones to the city
she's going everyday

to the Bamboo Garden
for a feed of fries
enjoyed more
when not thinking of
him who takes his grain to town
has his pigs hauled away
such exchanges
the village notes
while he returns
to only himself
the familiar trip home
on the washboard stretch
finding his lane
through the poplars and lilacs
to where he lives alone
and the old men of the village
shake their heads, wonder
what distractions
he creates during winter
if money holds him back
sometimes his pants so grimed
they're stiff
like a harness he'd throw
on a horse
the unspoken hope
that when he breaks
he'll drop in his field
not go
shooting the animals
and then himself
or coming into town
arguing about sugar

or tea, thinking
the price went up
only for him
the women get after their men
to be around
if necessary get Willie help
so the police don't come
and take him off his sandy lot

past the graves
of those who left
windows open one solo night
preparing for takeoff
leaving beef bones for the dog
still eating
next morning, marvelling
at the bounty
raising his head up
stuffed, a long dog
on the kitchen rug or in the beam
of the back door's merry dawn
his owner dreads
may bring
false hope . . .

the women and their connection
with eggs of hens, ducks, geese
carrying in their red hands
the delicate life
always close to the hurt thing first
the first to know

teaching us to reach under
the white warm feathers
their battle
when equipment
kills a son or father
in the fields
the baler high-listed
among foes, for days after
kids not in school
finally arrive
the older dragging the younger
shy to be back
the tall girl not so good
at third base as last year

mothers with the job
of holding broken parts

the way my aunt
kept Harvey upstairs
who never went
to school, his limbs
bent, a spider's
when you crush it
not yet dead
lived in bed
not often
in the living room
unless carried, an acrid smell
his eyes bright
his wool vest tight upon

a caved chest, everyone
fussing and weary
of the burden, and then he died
and people cried so much
because he seemed
not to have lived
his early death
foreordained, they all said
his box smaller than most
from the beginning
his fate
the weak and the runty
I had seen
lovingly
wrapped in flannel
and carried into the house
out of the cold barn
a box
behind the kitchen stove
their special smell
(chick or piglet)
tells us we were right to be
kind and yet they died
though we gave them names
one summer and into
the fall, all they had
before they climbed
the slimy stairs
into Fritz's truck
prodded by his stick
and hauled away

and returned much later
an envelope
(my father pondered
my mother scowled)
for the blood
shed by animals miles away
on a sawdust floor
in a shack near tracks
steam rising
men with knives and stunners
strapped to belts
farm boys . . .

        and yet
        elsewhere
others murmur and pat the tough rump
so the animal knows
who comes with love
at least one lad
leans against the barn door
and imagines
flying over lightning rods
the mint hayfields
a white horse
lifts him so he can see
where he began
and yet might be going
his hands entangled in mane

while young women
took up typing and filing and

catching the round bus
home to the flat
three cousins shared
each one after
a different man, hair stacked
up and waiting
on the dirty windy streets
they travelled on
away from the eyes of
aunts, and uncles who drank
silently while others
went loudly to the grave
preceding their parents
who carried them

to where fences meet
in the field (sand, not
good earth for growing)
set aside
by municipal fathers
now resident . . .

one skeletal husband
stood by the corn field
as long as one summer
while a wife burned her fat
away, never moving from her bed
afraid of the doctor
speaking fast
her own tongue thickening
her sons woollen
and silent by the door

coming to take her hand
all their eyes filling
except one raged
against his father who never
bought the dresses
his mother once wanted
but no more
past the worry
her heart softening
against that man
because she knew
he would follow her
one day in the potato patch
passing down into the black
worked and reworked soil
to taste the mineral that he was
sharp, iron, foreign
tiny crystal stones on his teeth
little white micas he had
combined with shit from the animals
and built rows of
raspberry canes, fences
buildings so tall
they needed rods even higher
to pull lightning
down around the walls
and into the blackened ground
much like the kind
his sons picked him up from
and then laid him back into
beside his wife
and where his sons took

families to trim and plant
disturb the fat snakes
sliding into spaces
at the edge of the grave
nearest their mother
where the headstone
most needed repair
and where they were beginning
not to believe the Biblical
phrases and consolations
chipped in granite . . .

to address death
cut deep in stone
the last words on the subject
not nighttime whimpers
(the pillow rolled away)

some of their words reach me
as I climb through the window
into the school
bunch of young boys and
one smart one
we went in
to cut up the flag in the
dark of the room
that had snared
too much of our clear light
dumped over desks
pulled at the secret shelves
of the lady teacher

and found soft stuff there
but no money
no secret letters
the strap
in the top drawer next
to the ledger of our days
which I thought momentarily
to alter by taking up
her favourite pen
innocent in its groove
adding x's to those girls
who never failed their teacher
and yet could inadvertently
bare a breast while breathing
over the hot math test
in June that final month
of short sleeves and
report cards coming home
and comments good or glaring
like those of the judge
after those of the school board
after teachers, store owners
other students, the janitor
first because he found
our crime and
the cop came driving in
from a farther town, his car
so long and heavy
a sword come down on us
we swore never to tell
Johnny Muzika went in first

sat in that seat
the cop taking down
words one by one
an infraction of interest
at last, young boys off their heads
and a leader to stir up
their little lives, make them
plan and smoke
break and enter
and no one would think of them
except everyone did
and turned us in
to face the magistrate
parents in their
Sunday clothes hoping
he would see them
not their sons
that the cop would say
these are good kids
first time
for him and him, hoping no one
would bring up the flag
at least not the way
the teacher raged
her word *sacrilege*
the story of a brother
killed on the Italian front
how we later
attached a rubbery safe
to the outdoor well
and pumped until the sack

swelled
miraculously unbroken by mass
hanging down from the spout
onto the well's cover
waiting for her
she howled
we watched with grim
admiration when she
found not me
not Ricky beside me
but cocky boy-man Delbert
and wore him down
the angle of her voice not the same
she used for reading Keats
(we never knew
urn yet loved it
finding in ourselves
what before had only been
jug)
she made him cry
he who was
so strong with us before
his shame
drew a line
but within a week
we were one gang again
and the hem on her skirt
stayed frayed, undone
her lipstick
expecting comment
not the late-in-life pregnancy

that took her out of our class
sent fathers into meetings
out of which they pulled
a young man who kept order

a fool for thinking
priceless meant cheap

got us through math
and handed us over
a Romanian émigré
twisted nose
French accent
smoked after 4:00
leaned back when he talked
the better to survey
squint and despise
how small we were
our parents fools
for placing us
in his trust
where I first learned
someone else
controls

   —communication handed down

from A. Dawn
Management in charge
for Hong Kong
that piece of paper
under my door

stepping lively so I don't
tread on it but then
wishing I had
besmirched it
faint dog spots

from the park
a five percent raise in the rent
oldsters rave in the hallway
afraid fixed incomes
will not do . . .

and as they rage
the boy beside me
shrinks
steps behind me
and his witnessing
begins to fade
I notice him less, reflect more

on impermanence
forgo attachment to
wood floor and view, so
he who puts up pictures
takes them down
driven by the lords of money
to another boxed space
to listen for
new neighbours, learn

who plays music, who slams
doors, which suite
parties, who smokes, who
smokes dope, who fries fish
on Fridays, who

dumps your laundry
on the floor, who screams
and puts up notes printed
in red felt-marker
whose lovemaking

wakes up two floors
was it Morency
Neudorf Garboui
Wilton Pasecreti Winch
gladdened for a morning

who loves his neighbours
let him open his hand
so we can crowd close and
examine what makes him
sweet-minded

—the boy remembers then
one evening
stepping onto the train to
Vancouver, the three of us
(Mum, Dad, me)
sat in coach seats and
marvelled
at the porter

offering his white-bread
sandwiches for a price
that shocked us into burrowing
through our bags
until such supplies ran out
and we awoke
from sore necks
to blue mountains and torrents
flashing under our wheels
and clouds caught on peaks
that offered now and then
banners of white
until we reached Hope
and sped past the long
green flat farms my father
admired long after
we reached the city itself
in rain

the veils that drift
in mist-held conifers
out of which drips spill
and grow ravens
dropping baritone stories
in a valley
where a kid isn't listening
too intent on imagining
elsewhere

and I looked and looked
to imagine the place
I would be living in later
but I skirted and missed
the near touching of

the young on the old
I could have looked
and seen him at a window
up in future light
no braces to hold

his pants, his head bare
without the toques
and caps and scarves
required by a mother's
love to fight off death

by cold and hail
and in his mind
(had I looked) some ghosts
dispatched while others
hungered on

like my father and
uncles before I was born
forced out
to find work and women
and spending hours
instead in the company
of men who built

the telegraph through
the Rockies, eventually
getting on with
Standard Oil, every day
a wet path down to the docks
men bent
in the photos
     —and bringing that rain
home to the fields
at the wrong time, between
seeding and haying, the grain
just up and seventeen days
of downpours
then high summer
dark green light green
from the road
up close it's alive
creeping eating
insects until we spray them
into death, long aluminum arms
reaching out from the
sac of poison strapped
to the tractor's back
clean downward blossoms
pass into the busy
bodies, the thin legs
crooked and no longer
springing into flight
the large jaws stilled
food for crows and flickers
later the snow

packing down their flexible
forewings, their membranous
underwings till they are soil
releasing themselves
and their agents
into the mass of humus
and bent molecules my father
ran through his hands
as if dirt would speak

the spring fires burn off
the crust of white stems
releasing the green shoot
up through the char
fresh smell of smoke

the night
the main block of town
burned down, row of
post office, lumberyard, café
and old store owned by
old people who were said
to be seen
getting on the 1:40
from Flin Flon
that night, two suitcases
he helping her
up into the car and the conductor
watching the flames
starting to leap
every piece of wood
crying out for its owner

Smitty
at the end of the row
half-mad for his small
granary-sized
barber shack
dragged in
a year before and plopped
at the corner to serve
those who needed a bowl cut
and some spittle on the skull
his only chance
at something he could do
his whole life
the old woman in
the Post Hotel saw the flames
across the street
and came out of her room
in her shuffling
slippers to cry
and shout at her husband
to hire more men
to hold back the fire
from the stuffed owls
in her front parlour
their glass eyes
under glass itself
overfilled with dread
reflecting heat
two horses in the livery
catch the smell early
kick at the stalls

and soon the shouting
of men's voices
coming out of their beds
their wives running and crying
some part of their lives
done for, Karen, her dad
her mum
good with people, their home
back of the café
next morning just black
a handful of suitcases
some chairs, clothes
piled across the street
as far as they got
without rushing back
for more until the heat said
no more, and the walls fall in
the ice cream scoops melt
the wallpaper sends up flames
from the floor to the roof
special acid reek of
linoleum's bubbling oil
every white napkin
every dispenser
the straws and glasses
the plywood partitions
and benches, gum
under the seats
and the ice cream cone
crumbs rolled under the hat rack
the jars of jawbreakers

rows of Players and Export A
cans of Copenhagen snuff
back rooms full of hot dog buns
Orange Crush

the roll call of catastrophe
the boy announces yet again
the event that ever after
marks the age
the fire of '52
the summer of seven hailstorms
the winter he learned to read . . .

and the street rebuilt
in brick, its age new
when I enter school
and become more myself
so fast the former world
is launched away into
dream light

where he stands tiny
by his mother's apron
his father's fly
and sees past
the crack in the screen-
door opening to a wide
porch or plain
of white
then green
sweet colours to those who love
land

      —and now down across the park
to the ravine's edge
of lawn and big fir and
Dead Man's Slope
two teenaged boys

cutting through the ravine
for a faster way home
discover a man
dead for several days
at press time nothing more

nameless homeless
dying in an urban dip
no one on the trails Sunday
not even dog walkers
afraid his ghost

will find them alone
and want his life back
in more than a *frisson*
from the place he died
under leaf and bough

the overhang huge
keeping the earth
dry from summer
where he stopped
for a rest, a cobweb

held his eye as its silver
line slid up and down
and finally up
beyond the gurgle
and the thump he left behind

I can tell the boy has seen death
on his own, it is not death
that will separate him from me
when I die
will he die too

maybe a minute later
catching up
and becoming me
one last little
togetherness

flowing back and forth
or will he wander on
with his smile
and his magical hands
trying his spell

on strangers
who brush past
maybe one or two turning
or stalling when
a shiver

touches
sad to think of
before going on
he makes dogs whine
and finally he sits down

on the end-of-summer grass
and waits
a boy like him must have
an angel who will come
the kind who comes only

to empty schoolyards
where the swing moves on its own
or he will turn into
another, some moment will
make him

solidly someone else
with a new name
driving himself each morning
against the air
in order to find

what he craves
until ultimately
nothing of him will be me
a little
murmuring

some sound
in the pesky dream
the old
pressures—he decides
in the morning light—

make no sense, half-strangled
urges leaping up inside
dogs lunging for treats
waves on the backs of
other waves

grass covering grass

from many years past
one blade and then another
and then a further
uppermost one, green growing
dryer, darker and
disappearing for a time
into mouse homes
and soil substrata

for the boy
I point out photocopiers
cellphones, the towers
even his spacey dreams
could not foresee
his house two storeys

the phone a party line
what needed copying
needed another hand
and more ink
not ballpoint pens

that smeared and ran
and were thrown away
in disgust by his father
these cars
much smaller than those

he longed to drive, girls
less clothed than those
he dreamt he danced with

the leaves of the maple
staining the sidewalk red
the neon, the fountain
the children wading
the quickly cashed cheques

the sidewalk flowers
blooming from their rubber pails
grown overnight
in the store
already at the pub

some patrons
the smell of beer
and wet cloths wafting
into the street, the same
dull looks

the man with his cigarette
and red face
easing into evening
the crush at the bus stop
the whoosh of diesel

expelled passengers
happy to get down
the sidewalk spattered in gum
and butts, the bank's
glass doors

asking us to keep still
till we reach the fresh face
of the teller we don't know
by name, the stories
on the mouth

of the lunging woman
too heavily made up
the man with his briefcase
left upper lip
snarling at air

the young boy
draped in chains
raising up a boom box
or else plugged in, the wire
snaking down to

some glint
cupped in his hand
the cars the trucks
the A-frame sandwich boards
announcing easy access

the sidewalk cafés
the writing on the wall
in Farsi
he reaches to touch
another world I explain

as best I can: upheaval
far away, thirty thousand
end up here, some rich
here in Irantown, mid-Lonsdale
the bakery, baklava

the barber
$12 a cut and the lesson
in history free, once
a math teacher
at a college in Tehran

he speaks fondly, loudly
grammatically incorrectly
of his life there, his wife here
his baby colicky
the hair of other men

their cowlicks and misery
his wild eye, his gold chains

and the boy recalls
airplanes dropping silver
strips he later found
in the fields
the communists poised
he heard
and when *Sputnik*
crossed over
some farmers
fondled guns

—but I cannot explain all that
clatter of long ago
and stop instead
and look him in the eye
and there between the rows

of plasticware from China
and the bus stop ads
for nakedness and chic
I draw out of him
his fright of any new
non-local paroxysms

unheard of till now
and feel it enter
a hard beat in me
heart gone gasping

wanting him to stay
the smiling innocent
at least till I explain
our pleasure in
double low-fat latté

the speed
with which we do
the business of business
from a coffee cup and cell
networking

laptops to NASDAQ
out of breath
I want to say
there's always more and more
but shout to him—as he moves
down the street and I move up—

to watch for the ferry
take the Seabus
when he smells the water
that's when he should
get on board

squeeze through
onto the Beaver
and by the time he reaches
the harbour's far side
he'll know enough

maybe to go home
to his classmates and his
pretty teacher:

the future hurries
so I couldn't hold it
though some
seemed to know
how to live

—and his friends will quiz him
and then give up
when he says he saw no
rockets, just more humans
than expected
though less wind
and more noise
and noise all night

where I'm on my own now

till the paperboy
throws his bundle
against my door, thunk
says hello

here's more
world shrunk down
to pages, photos of change
and I take my tea
to the window's
first light
and begin my wait
the eagle
screeching in his treetop

and far from me
the boy bobs and slides along
the last I saw of him
one of a crowd, his hair
sunburnt
touched by rain
the glimpse enough
to know he is holding
up the bones in me
through the distance
I've walked
from dawn light awakening
a child from his night

and I can see
I haven't left behind
what came with me

HAD I STAYED ON THE FARM

for Leona Gom

I married the skinny girl
and our kids ran free as chickens
one of them, the second boy
moving along the ditches for days
trapping muskrat and living on
chokecherries and bulrushes
sleeping by a little fire of sticks
wrapped in his jacket, and we hardly noticed
he was gone until he returned
as someone else, burnt and smoky
his sisters silenced by the strides he took
to reach the pump, the way he drank
from the barn well, his hands
a mesh of little nicks and cuts
where the cries of the animals
had entered him

I planted, and prayed
for the market to hold, and when
it failed I stopped praying
and never began again
found a fount of colourful
language when the truck broke
at harvest—and when the green straw plugged
the combine, I was the fool
who crawled in, it was my mackinaw
the flywheel caught and drove hard
into the iron guts of the machine
it was the mangled me my son
found, his mother he ran to
but even before he reached her

with the news she ever after
kept hearing, kept hearing
all the black suits of my neighbours
on their hangers
at the backs of the closets
began thirsting for sun and wind

I knew little of books
nothing of rhyme
though the rhythm
of spring, summer, fall
I replayed in winter
every day a time
for breaking down and
making each moment all
I needed, the snow filling up
space I might have stuffed otherwise
with words or lies or worse
falling until all was smooth
and white, virgin
cold
beauty I eventually forgot
to see, seeing instead
lives I might have lived
had I left, had I taken the train
not taken, riding with those
who later returned with ironic gleams
to look at me in wonder, the one
who stayed, as if only one were needed
to rate themselves against
measuring me as their fathers measured
fields of chaff and shrivelled grain

ABOUT THE AUTHOR

David Zieroth won the Dorothy Livesay Poetry Prize for *How I Joined Humanity at Last*. His poems have appeared in over thirty-five anthologies. He was born in Neepawa, Manitoba, and now lives in North Vancouver, BC. For more information, visit www3.telus.net/dzieroth.

ACKNOWLEDGEMENTS

"How I Came To Be" was originally published in *Grain*, and "Had I Stayed on the Farm" in *PRISM international*.

I am thankful for the support of the friends and writers who helped with this poem over the years, and I am especially grateful for the insights of Robert Adams, Meg Stainsby, Russell Thornton and Gillian Harding-Russell.